THE OAKWOOD PRESS

Fifty Years of the West Sussex Fire Brigade 1948-1998

by
S. Jordan

THE OAKWOOD PRESS

© Oakwood Press & S. Jordan 1999

British Library Cataloguing in Publication Data
A Record for this book is available from the British Library
ISBN 0 85361 549 7

Typeset by Oakwood Graphics.
Repro by Ford Graphics, Ringwood, Hants.
Printed by The Witney Press, Witney, Oxon.

Bosham Firemen putting out a stubble fire on the common in the early 1950s. The two boys by the pre-war Dennis fire engine seem to be getting a good ticking off, perhaps they know something about the fire.   *E.W. Wilson*

Front cover: Crawley's heavy rescue tender is fitted out for Special Services with persons reported trapped, i.e. road traffic accidents, collapsed buildings and son on. It mounts a HIAB crane on the back and has air bags, cutting gear and hydraulic rescue equipment.

Rear cover, top: Seen on the drill yard at Bognor are on the left a Bedford J5 and on the right is a Dennis F44.

Rear cover, bottom: A Mercedes Benz mountain range crash tender undergoing tilt testing at the Chobham vehicle test centre.

Published by
The Oakwood Press
P.O. Box 13, Usk, Mon., NP5 1YS.

Contents

Chichester's Volunteer Fire Brigade using hard suction to pump water from a pond, a scene from the early 1930s.   *R. Goodger*

A car and trailer pump detachment of the Bognor Regis AFS seen at a war bonds rally at Littlehampton early in the war.   *O.J. Cole*

I would like to thank all those, too numerous to mention by name, who have helped me in the production of this publication, especially all the serving and ex-serving members of the West Sussex Fire Brigade who have given me free run of their photo albums and memories. Special thanks go to my wife Sue who has diligently proof read all of my books to date, despite not always sharing my interests.

Introduction

The Fire Brigade in West Sussex has a long and meritorious history. Until the Watching and Lighting Act was passed in 1835 there was no legal requirement for towns and villages to provide a fire service; this did not, however, stop many towns in West Sussex providing their own 'parish pumps' or small manual fire engines which would be rushed to the scene of a fire by a team of willing volunteers - the earliest of these is Horsham's which was donated in 1780.

The Towns Police Clauses Act of 1847 gave provisions for the purchase of fire appliances, fire stations and the payment for firemen to crew them, all to be provided for out of the Poor Rates. By the turn of the 20th century there were town Brigades in Arundel, Bognor, Burgess Hill, Crawley, East Grinstead, Hassocks, Haywards Heath, Henfield, Hurstpierpoint, Littlehampton, Midhurst, Steyning and Worthing. Large estates such as Petworth House and Arundel Castle also had their own private Brigades.

Up until the mid-1930s the town Brigades continued to give sterling service, but the looming clouds of war with Germany caused the Government to create the Auxiliary Fire Service (AFS) in 1937. The AFS was formed to provide a cadre of trained, part time, Firemen to support regular Firemen fighting the deluge of fires expected from enemy bombing.

For the first two years of the World War II the local Brigades, with the help of the AFS, barely managed to cope with the massive workload caused by the Blitz. As time passed it became obvious to the Government that increasing organisational and supply problems could only be solved by providing a national command and control. To this end the Government decided to amalgamate all town and municipal Fire Brigades into one national organisation.

On 1st September, 1941 the National Fire Service was born, and West Sussex became part of Region 12 - Fire Force 32. However, the Government promised that this was only a wartime situation and that control of the Brigades would be returned to local councils once the war was over.

At war's end the town councils agitated for the return of their Fire Brigades. The Government, however, had seen the advantage of a large well organised fire service and was reluctant to return to the pre-war situation. As a compromise it was decided in 1946 that the control of Fire Brigades would become a County Council responsibility. West Sussex County Council set up a Fire Brigade Committee to oversee the transfer of power, this body held its first meeting on the 25th July, 1947. The chosen date for the formation of West Sussex Fire Brigade was the 1st April, 1948.

Fire Control Operators work at the operating panels in the Fire Control suite at Chichester, opened in 1965. *Author's Collection*

The new 'state of the art' Fire Control building opened in 1983 by HRH Princess Alexandra. *Author*

Fire Control and Communications

In the early days, your shout for help at a fire station would set bells ringing and small boys running to fetch the Firemen. By the turn of the century, and with the introduction of the National Telephone System, electric alarm bells were fitted in the homes of each Fireman which were operated by the flick of a switch at the fire station. These bells continued to be used through the 1940s and 1950s until they were replaced by sirens. In 1948 your 999 fire call would be intercepted by the local GPO operator who would alert the Brigade and set off the siren at the nearest fire station. One of the first acts of the West Sussex Fire Brigade (WSFB) was to set up a central Fire Control at Worthing. Once a call had been received the ladies of Fire Control could, by means of large scale maps, status boards and telephones, effectively control any incident calling out extra Firemen and appliances when needed. To enable even closer control to be exercised the Joint Police/Fire Service VHF Radio Scheme was set up. Using the VHF radio located at Worthing Fire Control voice contact was possible with appliances based at Horsham and Chichester. This scheme proved so useful that by 1959 twenty-four mobile stations were distributed around the county. During the 1950s direct 999 lines were set up by the GPO so that all fire calls were received by Fire Control. A series of callout systems for retained stations was set up, this involved Control alerting the nearest full-time station which would then call out the nearer retained station using a land line. In 1964 the callout system was upgraded by the introduction of the Post Office Remote Voice Frequency System 'A', this finally linked up all the county's fire stations to the central Fire Control at Worthing. The following year the Brigade were given their own VHF frequency and no longer had to share one with the police, also this year Fire Control and Communications moved into the brand new Headquarters building on St Pauls Road (now Northgate). The year 1976 saw the introduction of the PYE Pocket Phone 70 fireground radio. Crews could now be in direct communication with each other, or Fire Control, without returning to the fixed radio in the appliance. By the late 1970s Fire Control was not only outgrowing the office space allocated to it in the HQ building, the callout system was also becoming obsolete. A decision was made to upgrade the 999 callout system and to house it in a new, purpose built Fire Control building on the HQ site. By 1981 the building was complete and the installation of the new system had begun. The computerised system, designed by International Aeradio Limited, had been given the name of Firewatch and it came on line on the weekend of 26th/27th February, 1983. However, by 1991, due to the almost doubling of 999 calls over the previous eight years the Firewatch system had reached the limits of its capacity. Plans were therefore made to replace this system with a larger, quicker and more efficient one. After much consultation with the Home Office and suppliers the contract for the new command and control system was placed with Remsdeq. In July 1993 the Remsdeq Rescue computer went on line.

In 1995 new pagers were issued to all Retained Firefighters and full-time officers. This now enables Fire Control to call out whole crews or individual personnel at any time of the day or night. Fire Control operates a four watch continuous shift system to ensure that emergency calls are dealt with 24 hours a day. Each watch has an establishment of two Leading Fire Control Operators and three Fire Control Operators, supervised by a Senior Fire Control Operator. Fire Control staff are the primary point of contact for the public and in the year April 1996 to April 1997 they answered 21,050 emergency calls.

Ardsheal House, Worthing, the Brigade's first training centre.

Brigade Training Centre (BTC)

Although the Brigade does not provide initial training for its Firefighters, this is done at Eastleigh in Hampshire, it does provide all the follow-up training. Retained recruits are given all their training by BTC instructors.

The Training Centre was first set up in Ardsheal House, Worthing, but this building was later demolished to provide land for the construction of the new Worthing fire station and Divisional Headquarters. The Brigade Training Centre then moved next door to a converted house, to which classrooms and extra office space have been added at the rear.

In these lecture rooms Firefighters are given initial and refresher courses in the use of Bretahing Apparatus (BA), also promotion courses and examinations are carried out here for Junior Officers. In the drill yard is a Hot Box which gives Fire-fighters a realistic insight into the conditions to be found in a burning, smoke-logged building. First Aid and Fire Prevention courses are also taught at the centre.

A satellite centre at Tangmere houses the Brigade Driving School. At Tangmere Firefighters take HGV, Grade 'A' Driver, Defensive Driving and pump operator courses as well as Hydraulic Platform refresher courses. On the old airfield is a skid pan where drivers learn to control their vehicles in all weather conditions.

Firefighters learning first aid skills in the modern lecture room.   *Author's Collection*

9

Engineers at work on a row of Austin appliances inside the Brigade's workshops at St Pancras, Chichester, in the 1960s.

Brigade Workshops

The Brigade Workshops were first set up in 1948 in a small bay at East Preston fire station, but were moved in 1949 to larger premises at the rear of Chichester fire station. Unfortunately this site soon proved to be too cramped, also when it was cold or wet the mechanics suffered the full effects of the weather in the well ventilated and unheated building. In November 1956 the Under Secretary of State for the Home Office wrote that, 'over the past years work has been carried out under appalling conditions in temporary accommodation which forms part of the Chichester Cattle Market and which is quite beyond any form of repair'. Following the inspection of several sites the Workshops moved in 1957 to the former D. Rowe and Sons building on St Pancras, Chichester. This ex-garage was eminently suitable for use as the Brigade Workshops as the purchase price of £15,500 included all the tools and equipment, and so with very little alteration it was soon in operation for the repair, conversion and maintenance of the Brigade's fleet of appliances and cars.

In 1978 the Workshop Engineers again packed up and moved location. This time the location was a converted stores building on the old RAF airfield at Tangmere. The RAF had left this old Battle of Britain airfield and handed the site to the County Council at the same time as the St Pancras workshops were becoming too costly to maintain and redevelopment was threatening the site.

The Workshops are responsible for the safe running of all Brigade vehicles, and are able to carry out major repairs, resprays, overhauls and conversions in the well equipped workshops. All new appliances and officers' cars are fitted out at Tangmere before going 'on the run'.

In 1995 the high standards maintained by the engineers was rewarded with the award of ISO 9002 status. For minor repairs and maintenance the workshops have five mobile Service Van Engineers, based at Chichester, Worthing, Horsham and Haywards Heath.

The Brigade's workshops are now based on the old RAF airfield at Tangmere.
Author's Collection

11

Attending road traffic accidents (RTAs) to release trapped casualties is only one of the specialist tasks carried out by the Brigade. This photograph shows a rescue being carried out in 1964.

J.W. Percy

Burgess Hill Firefighters rescuing a sheep which has become trapped in a ditch.   *I. Henley*

Special Services

Apart from attending fires, as one would expect, Firefighters are called out to many other kinds of incidents for which their specialist training and equipment makes them ideally suited.

Road Traffic Accidents (RTA)

The Fire Brigade is called out to an RTA if a person is trapped in a vehicle following an accident and needs to be released without further injury. All front line fire appliances carry special hydraulic cutting and spreading equipment for removing doors and roofs from vehicles, as well as air bags for lifting heavy weights from trapped persons.

Animal Rescue

Animal rescue kits are held at three points within the county, Storrington, East Grinstead and East Wittering. These stations hold a range of large animal tackle which is used to extricate farm animals from slurry pits, ditches, wells, rivers or anywhere else they manage to become stuck. Personnel receive special training at Brinsbury College in the use of this equipment and in handling domestic farm animals. Certain rescues still require a large amount of ingenuity when normal rescue methods are not possible. At a recent rescue of 15 sheep from an underground pipe only two feet in diameter and 130 metres long, in a scene reminiscent of the film *The Great Escape*, a Fireman propelled himself along the pipe on the farmer's son's skateboard, grabbed a sheep and was then pulled back by his crew.

Planes and Trains

The Brigade is also called out to air and rail crashes where their expertise in casualty extrication comes into its own. Fortunately these events do not often happen, but in the 50 years the Brigade has existed there have been five major train crashes - Littlehampton in 1949, Ford Junction in 1951, Barnham Junction in 1962, Littlehampton again in 1963 and Christ's Hospital in 1964. The sighting of many post-war military training aerodromes in the area contributed to an unusually large number of aircraft crashes in the 1950s and 1960s during which time eight RAF or Royal Navy aircraft were lost in the county. As the air bases closed the aircraft crash landings became more civilianised in nature, the worst air disaster of all being on 4th November, 1968 when an Iberia Airline's 'Caravelle' aircraft, on route from Malaga to Heathrow, crashed into woods near Fernhurst - all 57 passengers and crew were killed in the impact and subsequent fire. The emergency services were heavily involved in this disaster, seven fire appliances and two service vans carrying emergency lighting, 16 ambulances, various Army units and all available Police were rushed to the scene but to no avail. In a later incident a trainee glider pilot forced landed into

A trainee glider pilot and her instructor from the Southern Gliding Club are rescued after crashing into power lines near Parham.   *Author's Collection*

woods near Parham House, the glider coming to rest precariously balanced on a tree and a high tension power line. Once the power had been turned off the Brigade was able to rescue the pilot and her tutor using a hydraulic platform.

Flooding

The powerful pumps fitted to fire engines make them ideal for all types of flooding incidents, from burst pipes and water tanks to major natural disasters. Most recently the Brigade were heavily involved with the devastating floods in the Chichester area during the winter of 1994/95, pumping out dozens of private homes and businesses and in the city centre crews pumped millions of gallons of water 24 hours a day for two weeks.

Chemical and Oil Spills

Each pump appliance in the Brigade carries a chemical and oil spill clean-up pack donated by the Environment Agency. The kits contain absorbent socks and granules, also pads and strips of a putty like substance used to block drains. Using these kits firefighters are able to mop up anything from a minor fuel leak or burst drum to major incidents like an overturned fuel tanker and stop the chemicals reaching the water supply. A quantity of larger chemical spill equipment is carried on the Incident Support Unit vehicle which can be rushed to the scene of an accident if needed.

Here is a list of the Special Services given during the year 1959/60; it would not matter which year one chose during the past 50 as the jobs would still be as varied as these:

Female person overcome by coal gas	1
Recovery of body from flooded gravel pit	1
Boy trapped in chimney pot	1
Male person attempting to jump from window	1
Assistance rendered to collapsed persons	3
Male trapped in sand hopper	1
Person trapped in car in pond	1
Male person trapped in tree	1
Release of trapped cattle or other animals	8
Persons locked in or out of rooms or premises	23
Leakage of dangerous gasses	2
Removal of petrol or harmful liquids from roadways	13
Storm damage, flooding, etc., to premises	33

The River Road fire station at Arundel was located in an old mill.

Arundel

In 1909 the Fire Brigade in Arundel consisted of five officers and 16 men, with a manual fire engine, a hand cart and 700 feet of hose. The fire station was behind the Town Hall in Maltravers Street. Arundel Castle also had its own private Fire Brigade which was much better equipped than the town Brigade, having two steam engines, two hose carts and 2,640 feet of hose. In the 1930s the town Brigade moved to new premises in a converted mill on River Road. Following the war Arundel became Station 22 of the West Sussex Fire Brigade.

It was, and still is, a retained station - manned only during emergencies - and was equipped with a Fordson lorry which towed a trailer pump and a Dennis Ace fire engine. These two appliances were replaced in 1954 by a Bedford S type fire engine. Although the River Road fire station had been upgraded in the 1950s it was still damp and hard to keep warm in the winter as it backed on to the River Arun. In 1967 a new single bay fire station was opened on the Ford Road.

Arundel is currently home for nine retained Firefighters under the command of a Station Officer, they are equipped with a Dennis SS WrL appliance.

The newly-opened fire station on Ford Road, Arundel.   *Author's Collection*

17

The fire station at Billingshurst, c. 1948, with an Austin towing vehicle in the garage.

Billingshurst

The current fire station at Billingshurst was opened in July 1953 and replaced an old wartime emergency station housed in a large wooden shed. The new one-bay station has a lecture room, watch room, muster bay and ablutions.

As an aid to training it was decided in 1973 to construct a drill tower at the station. In August 1974 the tender from a local company, J. Worman of Midhurst, was accepted to fabricate and erect a tubular steel drill tower at a cost of £11,074. Delays in obtaining the desired rolled steel tubing from the foundry, caused by a massive build programme in the North Sea oil rig industry, meant that a redesign was required to be able to use a different grade of steel in the construction. After long delays the fabrication and erection was carried out in February 1976.

Billingshurst is currently home to a Dennis DS153 WrL appliance manned by a retained crew.

The replacement fire station at Billingshurst opened in 1953.   *Author's Collection*

The Clarence Road, Bognor Regis, fire station was opened in 1939 and was not replaced until 1975 with the move to the present station on West Meads.
Author's Collection

Bognor Regis

This seaside resort had its first Fire Brigade in 1873 when the Bognor Volunteer Fire Brigade was formed. Initially the Brigade was equipped with a manual fire pump, but this was replaced in 1905 when a Shand Mason double vertical steam engine was purchased. In 1920 horses were replaced by horse power when an ex-War Department FWD lorry was equipped for firefighting duties and as the towing vehicle for the steamer.

After several homes the Brigade moved into new premises in Clarence Road. Originally designed as a two-storey building the onset of World War II meant that the second floor was never built and the accommodation was cramped from the start. By now the Brigade was equipped with a 1925 Leyland, 1934 Leyland FK1 and a 1937 Dennis emergency tender.

In 1949, shortly after its absorption into the WSFB, it was announced that Bognor Regis would have only a day manning crew instead of the full-time fire crew it then enjoyed. After many complaints from the town council and local residents the plan was shelved and the station remains to this day a 24 hour full-time cover fire station.

As the town grew, and holiday traffic increased and the shortage of accommodation at the old fire station became acute, it became obvious that the town centre station would have to be closed and a new one built on the outskirts of the town. Several sites were looked at but the chosen one was on a corner of the Grammar School campus on West Meads Drive.

The new fire station was officially opened in 1975 and is now the home for 36 full-time Firefighters, split into four watches, and 17 Retained Firefighters.

To enable the Firefighters at Bognor to respond to any type of emergency call there are six appliances stationed there, a Dennis Rapier F88 WrL, a Dennis SS WrL, a Landrover Series III 109 L4T and an Iveco Ford cargo truck. The two latest vehicles were introduced in 1997, they are a Dennis Dart bus chassis converted for use as an Operational Control Unit and a Mercedes-Benz Operational Support Unit carrying palletised equipment and a piggy back Moffet Mounty fork lift truck.

Wheeled escape drill at the Clarence Road drill yard, Bognor Regis.   *E.W. Wilson*

Bosham

Bosham was one of the first towns in West Sussex to have a new fire station built after the formation of the West Sussex Fire Brigade, the building being declared open in November 1953.

On 20th April, 1982 the local crew were called out to Petworth Cottage, Bosham. The roof was already well alight when they arrived at this large country house. Six BA sets, six jets and four hose reel jets were used during two hours of intensive firefighting. Water was drawn from a garden pond and an indoor swimming pool during the operation.

Later the same year the crew were called out to Southwood Farm to release a cow in calf from a Dyke. Animal Rescue gear and agricultural implements were used to facilitate the rescue, which lasted for more than an hour. In October 1998 the station was supplied with a new Dennis Rapier 411 fire appliance.

Opened in 1953 Bosham's fire station was one of the first new stations to be built by the new West Sussex Fire Brigade. In the background is the hose drying mast.

Author's Collection

Burgess Hill

In the late 19th century fire services in the Burgess Hill area were provided by the Burgess Hill and District Volunteer Fire Brigade from a fire station in the district council yard. In 1909 the Brigade, under Captain Sinnock, consisted of two officers and 10 men equipped with one steam fire engine, one hand escape and a hose cart with 1,520 feet of hose.

This Brigade was independently funded by local subscribers, the list in 1911 showed 208 entries totalling £73. In 1918 the Brigade became motorised with the purchase of a motor car to tow the steamer, the latter being replaced in 1923 with the acquisition of a motor fire engine. During the 1930s a second new motor appliance, a Dennis, was purchased.

In 1939 the Brigade lost its independence when it was taken over by the district council. Following war service in the NFS the Firemen found themselves, in 1948, forming part of the East Sussex Fire Brigade. The county boundary changes of 1974 saw the transfer of the town to West Sussex.

On 1st May, 1980 the Burgess Hill crew responded to an emergency call from the Cuckfield Parish Church, the spire of which was well alight. With the assistance of crews from Haywards Heath and Horsham damage to the body of the church was kept to a minimum; however, the spire was totally destroyed.

The tradition of local support in the town is still maintained, and a benefactor has provided the station with a thermal imaging camera, which is used to pinpoint hot spots in fires or trapped persons, and sees the retained crew called out to assist at many calls in the eastern half of the county.

Burgess Hill fire station. *Author*

23

Burgess Hill Firefighters attack a bungalow fire in the town.

I. Henley

Camelsdale

Opened in 1939 as a wartime emergency fire station Camelsdale was built on land leased by its first Station Commander, Mr Horace Green. The Nissen hut and wooden shed buildings were erected by the 36 men who enlisted as Firemen. Camelsdale is far up in the north-west of the county, in fact the Surrey/West Sussex border runs through the village. Midhurst is seven miles away to the west and Haslemere in Surrey is only ½ a mile distant.

The first appliance to be housed at the station was Mr Green's own Austin 18 motor car fitted with a towing hook for a trailer pump. Early in World War II this was replaced by a Bedford QL lorry which was itself soon replaced by two Austin ATVs. A second trailer pump was added to the inventory on the formation of the NFS in 1942.

On 1st April, 1948 Camelsdale became Station 20 of the West Sussex Fire Brigade and shortly afterwards the two Austin ATVs were replaced by a Dodge lorry converted for firefighting duties.

The Retained Firemen at Camelsdale covered a large rural area and so the majority of their calls were to farm and heath fires. In 1958 to assist the station in its off-road firefighting it was provided with a specially converted Landrover 109 fitted with a water tank and first aid hose. The following year the Dodge was replaced by a Bedford J5 water tender, and in 1960 the Landrover was replaced by a hardtop version.

By the mid-1960s falling call-outs and the proximity of the larger, and better equipped, fire stations at Midhurst and Haslemere brought the future of the station into doubt. In 1966 Camelsdale became the only fire station to close in the 50 year history of the Brigade.

Camelsdale fire station soon after its transfer to the West Sussex Fire Brigade in 1948.
Author's Collection

A Leyland and a Dennis F8 pose in front of Chichester's cattle market fire station.

J.W. Percy

Chichester

The City of Chichester can boast one of the oldest fire services in the county, second only to Horsham. In 1790 the City Council provided a building for Fire Brigade use, although by 1872 the equipment housed there consisted of only a hose cart and a few old lengths of leather hose. The situation improved in the 1880s with the purchase of a 32 man manual fire pump, two teams of eight men on each side. This pump and other equipment were not, however, well maintained and at an incident in September 1897 proved to be next to useless. Edney's department store on East Street caught fire and was totally destroyed, it was only with the help of the Bognor Brigade and soldiers of the Royal Sussex Regiment stationed in the city that the fire was put out. In 1905 a steam fire engine was purchased second-hand from the private Fire Brigade at Slindon House. The Brigade became mechanised in 1921 with the purchase of a motor lorry to tow the steamer, and in November 1923 a Leyland motor fire engine was delivered.

The old fire station in East Gate was closed in December 1926 and new premises in the Cattle Market were occupied. In July 1933 the old steamer was sold for £5 and a Merryweather tender pump and trailer were purchased from the Cowdrey Estate; the old 1870s hand cart was still in use during World War II. In the first year of its existence the WSFB replaced the oldest of the city's fire engines with a brand new Commer water tender fitted with a two way radio set which enabled it to be in contact with Fire Control, then located in Worthing.

November 1965 saw the opening of a new combined fire station, Fire Control and Brigade Headquarters on the Northgate roundabout. Chichester is currently home for a Dennis Rapier WrL, a Dennis SS WrL, a Mercedes 1124 Heavy Rescue Tender and a Ford 1700 BA Support Unit.

Chichester's Station 17 and Fire Brigade headquarters building. *Author*

Originally the home of the Crawley Volunteer Fire Brigade, this building had to be replaced when the town's population outgrew these small premises. *Author's Collection*

Crawley

The 1909 Sussex County Handbook informs us that the Crawley Volunteer Fire Brigade consisted of five officers and 14 men equipped with two manual fire engines and 1,430 feet of fire hose. The fire station was on Ifield Road. In 1920 a motor fire engine was purchased. When, in 1932, the Brigade was taken over by the Crawley, Ifield, Ringmer and Worth Joint Fire Protection Committee the equipment available had risen to a motor appliance and a motor tender with trailer pump.

The administration of the Brigade changed again in 1939 when the Horsham District Council assumed responsibility. After the war the Government began a massive building programme to house blitzed families, several 'New Towns' were built and Crawley was one of these. The local population exploded and the fire cover for the town also had to increase.

In 1956 a new three-bay fire station was opened and the manning was changed from retained to full-time, 24 hour, cover. On 4th April, 1958 the duty watch received a call to the New Era factory. Part of the premises was used for joinery and domestic hardware manufacture and it was this which was on fire. Quick work by all three Crawley pumps soon had the fire under control, damage was confined to some timber and several woodworking machines. The cause of the fire was attributed to a carelessly discarded cigarette end or a naked light setting fire to a pile of wood shavings and sawdust.

Before the fire station at Horley came under the control of the WSFB in 1981, Crawley was the first response station for Gatwick Airport.

Crawley Firemen on parade outside the new fire station in 1956.   *Author's Collection*

29

G.E.H. Peck

East Grinstead's Edwardian volunteer Fire Brigade pose proudly in front of their manual fire engine.

East Grinstead

The volunteer Fire Brigade formed in East Grinstead in the 1880s was taken over by the Urban District Council in 1894. The fire station was at 140 London Road, and by 1909 it was home to three officers and 19 volunteer Firemen, one manual fire engine, two hose carts and 1,300 feet of hose. The Brigade also had a smoke helmet, unusual for a small town Fire Brigade in these early days.

In 1948 East Grinstead was still a part of East Sussex and so the town Brigade first became a part of the East Sussex Fire Brigade. A new three-bay fire station was opened in 1967 and in 1974, following county boundary changes, responsibility for the towns fire protection was passed over to the WSFB.

On the night of 21st February, 1981 the Brigade was called to a fire in the Olde Felbridge Hotel. The first crew to arrive was that of East Grinstead. The hotel was full of guests and party-goers and several hundred people had to be evacuated before fire fighting could begin in earnest. Despite the best efforts of the East Grinstead crews, with the help of others from Surrey, Kent, East and West Sussex, the hotel was badly damaged. About half of the building was saved and there were no casualties among the staff or guests.

East Grinstead fire station is worked on the day manning principle, this means that full-time Firefighters man the station during normal office hours - but at night or weekends the Firefighters respond to emergencies from their homes - which are all close by the station.

East Grinstead's fire station, opened in 1967 whilst un...

East Preston fire station, before the addition of the two-bay appliance room in the 1970s.

Author's Collection

East Preston's converted barn fire station.   *Author's Collection*

East Preston

Situated on the coastal strip between Littlehampton and Worthing the retained station at East Preston is housed in a converted Sussex barn. Later the station was improved with the building of a two-bay appliance room on the south wing. The old appliance bay was converted to a lecture room.

In 1974 it was proposed to improve the station with the construction of a drill tower. The rising cost of suitable steel tubing, combined with a drop in available resources in the County Council's budget meant that the go-ahead for the build was not given until 1984. The contract was given to John G. Snelling and the tower was finally constructed in 1985 at a cost of £29,107.

East Preston is currently home to a 1991 Dennis SS WrL and a 1997 Dennis Rapier.

East Preston's volunteer Firemen pose beside their Austin towing vehicle in this 1948 photograph. *Mr Prole*

This 1953 view shows the East Wittering fire station after its wartime conversion from an Electricity Board showroom.

East Wittering

In 1933 two brothers, Jim and Jack Steel, began a small local Fire Brigade in the village of East Wittering on the Manhood Peninsular. They began by using the cast-off equipment from local Brigades, such as the 50-year-old hose cart from Selsey, which they refurbished themselves.

Just prior to World War II the Brigade was put on a more formal footing with the formation of an AFS branch at East Wittering. On the formation of the NFS in 1941 the local Electricity Board offices were commandeered for use as a fire station.

After 1st April, 1948 the WSFB kept open the station to provide fire cover for the Manhood Peninsular and the electricity offices were converted to a single pump retained fire station.

The crew is kept busy fighting fires and answering calls to the many holiday and retirement homes in the area. With the increase in boating in the Chichester and Bosham harbours it became apparent that some sort of fire and rescue craft was required in the area. In 1994 the appliance bay was modified to allow a Land Rover towing vehicle to park behind the pump, and an inflatable boat - powered by a 25 horse power outboard motor - is housed in a purpose-built boat house at the rear of the station.

East Wittering's fire and rescue craft in action on Chichester harbour.   *T. Tadd*

The pre-1966 fire station at Findon. The callout siren can be seen in the background.

Author's Collection

Findon

On 18th November, 1958 the Findon crew were called out to a fire at Wall's Stores, a local general store. The building, about 30 ft x 50 ft, was severely damaged and about 25 per cent of the stock was destroyed. With the help of a crew from Worthing they were able to prevent the fire from spreading to adjoining properties.

In 1961 the wooden shed previously used as a fire station was replaced with a brand new, purpose-built fire station with direct access to the A24. The crew is regularly called out to accidents on this busy dual carriageway.

Findon, just three miles to the north of Worthing town centre in a rural area of the South Downs, has had a major problem justifying the provision of a fire station in the village. Situated within a triangle of fire stations made up of Worthing, Storrington and Steyning, all able to respond quickly to incidents in the Findon area, the local Parish Council has had to fight long and hard to keep the fire station open. In the mid-1970s Government spending cuts reduced the Fire Brigade's budget to such a degree that closure of the fire station became almost the only option to balance the books. However, at the last minute cuts were made in other County Council departments and the station was saved.

The new fire station at Findon, built in 1961 as a replacement for the old wooden garage.
Author's Collection

Haywards Heath

The Haywards Heath and District Volunteer Fire Brigade was formed in 1889. Because the town had a newly laid water main, with sufficient pressure, it was deemed reasonable to equip the Brigade with only a hose cart and fire hose. In 1909 the Brigade, under Captain Clarke, consisted of two officers and eight men with the use of two hose carts and 1,250 feet of hose. In the early 1900s the old fire station was closed and the Firemen moved to new premises on South Road.

By the mid-1920s a new motor fire engine had been purchased and the Brigade was able to answer calls outside of the town main area. In 1934 a second appliance, a Leyland pump ladder, was purchased. Following wartime service in the NFS the Brigade was returned to local control in 1948 when it became part of the East Sussex Fire Brigade. In January 1962 a new fire station was opened on Mill Green Road, on the site of an old gasworks.

Following boundary changes in 1974 Haywards Heath became part of an enlarged West Sussex and all fire services were taken over by the WSFB. On 3rd June, 1978 the Brigade responded to an emergency call from W.C Hilton & Sons. The Haywards Heath crew saw that the fire in this factory could quickly get out of hand and raised the number of pumps in attendance to six. Firefighters using BA, hose reel and foam branches stopped the fire so quickly, and with so little damage, that the following morning staff were able to carry on their work unaffected.

Haywards Heath is only one of two day manning stations in the county. This means that full-time Firefighters are on duty at the fire station during normal working hours, but at night or weekends they respond from their homes.

A Dennis SS WrL stands outside Haywards Heath fire station.   *Author's Collection*

Henfield

The Edwardian complement of the Henfield Volunteers was two officers and 14 men equipped with one manual fire engine, a hand cart and 850 feet of hose. In 1936 a new fire station was built for the brigade and a Dennis motor pump appliance was purchased.

In the early 1950s plans were made to build a new, two-bay fire station. However, due to space and budgetary restrictions the plan was reduced to a rebuild of the existing one-bay station. The original appliance bay was converted to a lecture room and a new garage and watch room was built at a cost of £3,729.

On 19th September, 1956 the Henfield crew were called to a fire at Northview Cottage, Blackstone. On arrival the Firemen found that there had been an explosion at the rear of house which had blown out much of the rear wall and only a small fire which had burnt itself out. A woman with severe burns to the hands and face was conveyed to hospital. The Brigade shored up the floors and sheeted the rear of the house. The cause of the explosion was attributed to an open valve on a Calor Gas bottle and a concentration of gas being ignited by a naked flame.

In July 1982 a flashover occurred in the roof space of the Pidgeon Croft, Henfield. The fire was started whilst soldering work was being carried out with a blow torch. The local crew responded, but the fire destroyed the roof and 75 per cent of the first floor.

The 1936 fire station at Henfield which was incorporated in the new station as the lecture room.   *Author's Collection*

Henfield fire station after the 1951 rebuild.   *Author's Collection*

Old Horley town Fire Brigade.   *G.E.H. Peck*

Horley

Although part of West Sussex since the county boundary changes in 1974, the Horley fire station was manned and administered by members of the Surrey Fire Brigade until 1981. The 1974 boundary changes included the whole of Gatwick Airport in West Sussex and this produced the anomaly of Horley fire station, which was outside of the town on the airport periphery, being in West Sussex whilst the town itself remained in Surrey.

The situation was resolved in 1981 when a new retained fire station was opened in Horley town and the original fire station was handed over to West Sussex Fire Brigade control. The main purpose of the station, only a few miles from Crawley, is to provide emergency cover for Gatwick Airport. The station's appliances can be at an incident in moments, backing up the British Airport Authority's own internal fire service.

Horley fire station, erected by Surrey Fire Brigade and taken over by West Sussex Fire Brigade in 1981.   *Author*

Old Horsham fire station on North Street with a wartime Austin and two Fordson fire appliances in the garages.

Horsham

The town of Horsham has had its own fire service since 1780, in that year Lady Irwin donated a manual fire engine to the parish. Sixty years later the Horsham Volunteer Fire Brigade was formed and a band of trained men were now available to fight fires in the town. In 1908 the Brigade became mechanised with the purchase of a Shand Mason steam fire engine. The Brigade moved in 1930 from its original address on North Street to a new building further down the road on a site now occupied by the town library.

Following the formation of the WSFB in 1948 Horsham became the Headquarters of 'B' Division, which covered the eastern and northern half of the county.

By the mid-1960s fire appliances were getting bigger, also the work of the Divisional Headquarters was increasing and more office space was needed. The Brigade had obviously outgrown the North St site and so plans were made to build a new combined fire station and Divisional HQ. The chosen site was in Hurst Road where the Fire Brigade would share the premises with the Police, Ambulance service and Law Courts.

The new fire station consists of a single-storey three-vehicle appliance bay with added garages for specialist vehicles and a small workshops. Joined to this is a two-storey office block , the ground floor of which is given over to the fire crews with office and sleeping accommodation. The first floor provides office space for the Divisional Headquarters. In the yard is a drill tower and a heat and smoke chamber for breathing apparatus training.

The new Horsham fire station, opened in 1968.   *Author's Collection*

Hurstpierpoint

In 1909 Chief Officer J. Pearsey presided over the two officers and 14 men who made up the Hurstpierpoint Volunteer Fire Brigade. They were equipped with one manual fire engine, a hose cart and 1,100 feet of hose.

In 1948 the station came under the control of the East Sussex Fire Brigade, who rebuilt the fire station in 1962. The county boundary changes of 1974 put the town firmly in West Sussex and the crew transferred to the West Sussex Fire Brigade.

On 30th November, 1979 the Hurstpierpoint crew were called out to Goldbridge House, a large two-storey dwelling. On arrival they found the first floor was well alight. Within half an hour it became obvious that the fire was beyond the local crew and the call 'make pumps six' was sent to Fire Control. Firefighters using eight BA sets, two jets and three hose reel jets from two light portable pumps, pumping from a stream and a swimming pool, were used to extinguish the fire.

Hurstpierpoint fire station, opened in 1962.   *Author*

Keymer

The fire station at Keymer was built in 1937 by public subscription, it is a single-storey brick building with a tiled roof, originally outside it had a siren on a tower and two telegraph poles with a cross member for use as a hose dryer. The land on which the station was built, which was originally leased, was purchased by the East Sussex County Council in 1953.

The East Sussex Fire Brigade was always concerned that the size and location of the station were wrong and that a new station would have to be built in the Keymer area. A combined report of 1969 by the Fire Brigade Committee, Her Majesty's Inspector of Fire Services and the County Fire Officer stated that all three were of the opinion that the present fire station was inadequate for the following reasons: it was difficult to accommodate a modern fire appliance in the cramped garage; there were no drill facilities on site, no lecture/recreation/ drying rooms or showers; the location of the station on a road junction made answering emergency calls dangerous. It was decided that the station, presently located on the junction of Lodge Lane and Dale Avenue, should be closed and a new one built in the Keymer area. Among the many sites proposed for the new fire station was some agricultural land off Lodge Lane, an area of under-utilised allotments to the rear of houses in Windmill Avenue and Parklands Road, beside the Telephone Exchange on Windmill Avenue and on a playing field behind Stafford House.

Many further sites were looked into but all were rejected for one reason or another. A 1972 WSFB study of the fire cover for the area to be handed over to West Sussex in 1974 concluded that the station should be closed and that the ground should be covered by Burgess Hill fire station once it had been upgraded to a full-time station. The retained crew at Hurstpierpoint would respond as second pump to any calls in the Keymer area.

Following the County Council boundary changes in 1974 the West Sussex Fire Brigade decided not to close the fire station, but to continue the search for a new site within the Keymer area. This met with as much success as the East Sussex endeavours and so a programme of improvements was put into place. The much modernised building now has appliance bay, lecture room, kitchen, separate shower and toilet.

Keymer fire station. *Author*

Firefighters attacking the blaze at the Datsun premises, Lancing.

Lancing

In 1908 a volunteer Fire Brigade was formed by Lancing Parish Council, this consisted of eight men with a hose cart. Later a Baco Ford fire engine was purchased second-hand from Hove Fire Brigade and housed in a builder's hut. In 1925 a new fire station was built on South Street and this served the town throughout the war years and well into the WSFB era. A new fire station was opened on Elm Grove on 18th April, 1961 by the Chairman of the County Council as part of the modernisation of most of the fire stations in West Sussex during the 1960s. When the Brigade took over Lancing in 1948 the station complement was two old wartime towing vehicles and two trailer pumps, it was the gradual replacement of these old trucks by larger, more efficient ones, that was the trigger for providing the new fire station as the old one was just too small.

Immediately behind the Lancing fire station is the old London, Brighton and South Coast Railway Carriage Works; long since converted to factory units this became the site of the largest fire that the Lancing Firefighters have had to deal with. In 1973 the premises of Datsun UK caught fire and soon became well alight. The blaze was fought by over 100 Firefighters and it was not until the following day that the fire was eventually extinguished.

Lancing fire station, opened in 1961.   *Author's Collection*

The first Maltravers Road fire station with an Austin Escape parked in the garage.

Author's Collection

Littlehampton

The *Littlehampton News* of 24th July, 1875 tells us that the Littlehampton Volunteer Fire Brigade 'turned out for dry and wet drills with their large engine Tuesday last'. Their uniforms were dark blue with red and yellow facings, Captain Butt wore a large silver helmet and the men forage caps - although they had brass helmets for duty. In 1909 the Brigade consisted of Captain Constable, six officers and 19 men. They were equipped with two manual pumps, two hand escapes, two hose carts and 1,500 feet of hose, the fire station was next to Beach Road. The towns first motorised fire engine was purchased in the early 1920s, and a new fire station in Maltravers Road was built.

In 1939 a full time Chief Officer was appointed. During the latter stages of World War II the Littlehampton area was very busy with vessels forming up for the invasion of Europe; during this time two fire boats - *Windswept* and *Pride of Bognor* - were on duty in the harbour.

In 1968/9 a new two-bay fire station was built on the Maltravers Road site and it became operational in July 1969. Parts of the old station were retained and a Ford water carrier is garaged in the old appliance bay, also at Littlehampton are a Dennis Rapier WrL and a Dennis SS WrL.

Littlehampton is one of the busiest retained stations in the county and has answered an average of 710 calls per year for the last five years.

Littlehampton's new two-bay fire station, opened in 1969.   *Author's Collection*

Market Square fire station, Midhurst, the garage door of which has been widened to accept larger appliances. *Author's Collection*

The Wharf fire station at Midhurst was in use between 1953 and 1970. *Author's Collection*

Midhurst

The Midhurst Volunteer Fire Brigade was formed in 1865. At this time the brigade had two manual fire appliances, which were kept in a building behind the town gaol in Market Square. Later the Brigade moved into the gaol itself with the two cells being used as stores and workshops, and the Police Court upstairs being used as accommodation for the Firemen. In an unusual show of dedication the members of the Brigade voted in the early 1900s to use money earmarked for the annual dinner to be spent on new uniforms.

The horses for the appliances were kept in a field at St Anne's Hill, close to the station. These were finally put out to grass when the Rural District Council purchased a French Delauney Belleville four-cylinder fire engine. This appliance had solid rubber rear tyres and steel studded front wheels. When it first arrived at Midhurst the rather embarrassed town dignitaries found that it was too large to fit through the doors of the fire station. Extensive works had to be carried out to the premises, including lowering the floor by two feet and widening the doorway, before the appliance could be stabled safely in the building.

The Delauney was replaced in 1934 by a Leyland Cub, which was still going strong in 1948 when the Brigade was absorbed into the new WSFB. In 1955 the fire station was moved to new premises at the Wharf, Midhurst.

The ground that Midhurst had to cover was greatly increased in 1966 when Camelsdale fire station was closed. Midhurst Firefighters found they now had about 80 square miles of mainly rural countryside to cover.

The fire station at the Wharf proved to have some disadvantages, with traffic congestion being one of the major faults. A new fire station was built at the edge of town on New Road, this became operational on 26th October, 1970. When it first opened the station held a Dennis D Series WrTL, a Land Rover pump and a Land Rover ladder appliance. Currently serving at the station are a Dennis DS WrL, a Dennis Rapier TF202 WrL and a Land Rover Series III 109 L4T.

In 1970 this new two-bay fire station was opened in Midhurst. *Author's Collection*

The brick garage at Partridge Green, replaced in 1962.   *Author's Collection*

Partridge Green

For the first 14 years of the West Sussex Fire Brigade's existence Partridge Green Firefighters made do with a brick garage for a fire station, but in 1962 they were rewarded with a new fire station.

Partridge Green Firefighters wearing protective clothing and Breathing Apparatus sets had to deal with four gallons of Nitric acid which had leaked from a 20 gallon drum at the premises of Azureglen Ltd in 1982. The spilled acid was soaked up using an inert substance and the leaking drum was removed to the open air pending removal. Four of the factory workers were taken to hospital after inhaling the fumes.

On 6th February, 1986 the local crew were called out to nearby Swains Farm where the roof of a large timber framed farmhouse was on fire. The roof was clad with large slabs of Horsham stone but the strength of the structure was such that although the roof collapsed damage was confined to the attic. Using BA, the Partridge Green crew searched the smoke-logged house for 'persons reported', but none were found. Five jets were used to control the fire and prevent it spreading to the two other wings of the house. Whilst the fire in the roof was being tackled other Firefighters worked underneath to remove property from the house. Water was pumped from a nearby farm pond to supply the five jets used in the incident.

The modern single-bay fire station opened at Partridge Green in 1962.

Author's Collection

Petworth fire station, as taken over by the WSFB in 1948.

Petworth

The earliest record of a Fire Brigade at Petworth comes from 1895 when it was agreed that the Parish Council would pay a sum of money annually to maintain the fire truck and hose, although it is probable that this equipment was in use well before this date. By 1920 the Brigade had become mechanised by the purchase of a Model T Ford fire engine.

In 1935 responsibility for the Brigade devolved on to the District Council and the fire station was moved out of its old home at the town hall to a new location next to the town mortuary. By the late 1950s this building was becoming hopelessly inadequate and a new site had to be found. The place chosen was on a piece of ground next to the old Garland photographic studios. Now instead of an old shed the Petworth Retained Firemen had a smart new, purpose-built fire station which was opened on 27th June, 1961.

The main part of the station is the two-bay garage housing a Dennis Rapier WrL, a Dennis DS WrL and a Land Rover 4x4, off this are watch room, store room, kitchen, lecture room, ablutions and drying room. At the rear of the station is a drill yard with a practice tower.

The station has a major responsibility for the protection of Petworth House and many exercises are held to ensure the safe removal of art treasures in case of a fire at this historic building.

Petworth fire station opened in 1961.   *Author's Collection*

This was Selsey's fire station up until 1964, a Bedford van and appliance occupy the garages.
Author's Collection

Opened in 1964 Selsey's new fire station was later improved with the addition of a drill tower and a side bay for a Land Rover.   *Author's Collection*

Selsey

Located on the tip of the Manhood Peninsular, Selsey has been served by local men trained as Firefighters since 1910 when a volunteer Fire Brigade was formed.

Just before midnight on 29th November, 1961 a fire was reported in the Marine Hotel, Selsey. The local Firefighters turned out and found that the ground and first floors were well alight. Crews from East Wittering, Chichester and Bognor Regis were called in to help fight the fire. Due to high winds the conditions inside the building quickly became life threatening, and at 00.30 all the Firefighters working inside were withdrawn. Sparks were blown far from the seat of the fire by the high winds and threatened to set more fires and a Land Rover was used to race from site to site extinguishing embers. Despite preventing the spread of the fire to other nearby premises the Firefighters were unable to save the hotel.

Many of the local dwellings are thatched and the Selsey Firefighters have been called out to many thatch fires, notably those in 1951, 1953, 1958, 1959 and 1960, mostly caused by sparks from chimneys. In 1986 another thatched building, the Selsey Press premises, was attacked by fire. The roof was destroyed and the building and contents were damaged when the roof collapsed. Several nearby residents had to be evacuated because of the intensity of the fire.

Selsey's new fire station, on the High Street, was opened in December 1964 replacing an old tin shed. It is currently home for a Dennis Rapier and a Land Rover 4x4.

Fire at the 'Thatchings', James Road, Selsey, 21st March, 1958.　　　　　*J. New*

Old Shoreham fire station, Butts Road, Shoreham.

Shoreham-by-Sea

Prior to World War II Shoreham was in the favourable position of having two Fire Brigades, one maintained by the Shoreham-by-Sea Urban District Council adjacent to the council offices, and the other by the Southwick UDC in garages in Butts Road. Following the formation of the NFS in 1941 the two Brigades were merged at the Butts Road site and the premises enlarged with the building of several plasterboard sheds.

Bill Foss, a Fireman on Red Watch, recalls some early memories of the WSFB at Butts Road: Retained Fireman Ted Page, known as Frisby Dyke - dim as a NAAFI candle - was caught out on a practice night call. In those days Firemen had to dress standing on the running board of the old Dennis open appliance hanging on as best as they could. Frisby let go with both hands to pull up his overtrousers just as the vehicle turned a corner, and ended up in a bundle in the road. Later, at another practice turn out, called by the same officer, Divisional Officer 'Biff' Baker, Frisby decided to dress before mounting the appliance. This time, in his haste, he became tangled with his braces trapped in his crotch and the fire engine left without him. The crew returned to find 'Biff' consoling Frisby and trying to disentangle him.

On 1st January, 1949 Shoreham responded to a call to the nearby Toll Bridge, there they found a double-decker bus had left the road and was lying in the River Arun with its engine running and the lights still on. Eleven people were rescued from the bus without further injury.

On December 1954 the station was moved from Butts Road to new premises in Stoney Lane. Following the station's official opening, on Saturday 14th May, 1955, a display was put on by the brigade for the assembled crowds. The display consisted of a hook ladder drill, an oil fire, the AFS in action, turntable ladder drill and a fire scene.

The year 1981 proved to be a memorable year for the Shoreham crews with the potentially explosive MV *Frisian Star* tying up at Shoreham Harbour. For three days the crews stood by in case of fire or explosion in this bulk chemical carrier which had toxic and flammable fumes leaking from a container.

Shoreham is currently home for 32 full-time and 14 Retained Firefighters. Based here are a Dennis SS WrL, a Dennis Rapier WrL, a Dennis DF133 foam tender and a Land Rover series III 109 L4T.

The smart new fire station opened on Stoney Lane, Shoreham, in 1954.   *Author's Collection*

Steyning's manual fire engine and crew outside the old fire station.

G.E.H. Peck

Steyning

Steyning's Volunteer Fire Brigade first come to notice in 1904 when they helped put out a fire at nearby Knepp Castle; by 1909 the Brigade consisted of Chief Officer J. Tichener, two officers and 16 men. They had the use of one manual fire engine and a hose cart. In 1925 the Brigade became mechanised with the purchase of a motor fire engine.

The Steyning crew had to respond to a callout to the White Horse Hotel in the early hours of the morning of 20th March, 1949. The fire was discovered by a guest, who raised the alarm, he and the staff escaped without injury. With the assistance of four other crews and a turntable ladder the Steyning crew brought the fire under control; although the Firefighters stopped the flames spreading to nearby premises the hotel was severely damaged.

Another big fire occurred in the area almost 10 years later when fire was reported at the Spring Grove Laundry on 25th November, 1959. The premises, comprising two floors and a basement, were found to be well alight, and although the Henfield water tender was called out at the same time as the Steyning crew it soon became obvious that more help would be needed and pumps from Shoreham, Storrington and Partridge Green were called to the scene. The building and contents were severely damaged by fire, heat and collapse. The cause was later determined to be arson.

In March 1961 the weather-boarded premises used as a fire station was closed and a new single-bay fire station was opened.

The single-bay fire station opened in Steyning in 1961 to replace the old weather-boarded building. *Author's Collection*

The 1925 fire station at Storrington following its enlargement in 1930.

Storrington

The town Fire Brigade in Storrington was formed in 1922 by the local Parish Council, it was equipped with a manual fire engine and hose. In 1925 a new fire station was built in West Street and a second horse-drawn manual fire engine was purchased, this was replaced in 1928 when the town purchased a 17-year-old Fiat motor fire engine from Brighton Fire Brigade. The fire station was enlarged in 1930 so that it could accommodate two fire engines and a Dennis pump escape was purchased to assist the ageing Fiat.

In 1948 the Brigade was absorbed into the new WSFB. By the late 1950s the West Street station was past its prime and as part of the county modernisation policy a new station was built on the High Street, this being opened in May 1958.

In December 1981 the Storrington crew was called to a fire at the premises of Consumer Products Ltd, and found the central section of the works well alight with flames breaking through the roof. Used as a warehouse to store cosmetics, the building had large quantities of aerosol cans and a number of LPG cylinders inside. With the assistance of crews from 10 other stations the Storrington Fire-fighters were able to stop the fire from spreading to other parts of the premises. At the height of the fire 10 jets and 22 sets of BA were in use simultaneously.

This station's location, close to the Arun valley and the flood plains at Amberley and Pulborough, made it the ideal place to locate one of the Brigade's two inflatable boats; this has seen a great deal of use - especially for rescuing stranded animals.

Opened in May 1958 Storrington's fire station has two appliance bays and a drill tower.
Author's Collection

Turners Hill

Turners Hill can lay claim to having the most picturesque fire station in the county, it is an old converted blacksmith's forge - originally built in 1919, with a two-storey extension erected in the 1940s. The building is owned by the Paddockhurst Estate and is leased to the Fire Brigade. Apart from some modernisation work in the 1980s the interior is very much as it was in the immediate post-war period.

This station is one of those taken over in 1974 from the East Sussex Fire Brigade following the county boundary changes.

In 1981 the original lease expired and Paddockhurst Estates served a notice to quit on the Fire Brigade, efforts were made to relocate the station in the Crawley Down area but due to the prohibitive costs involved and local opposition the scheme was dropped and a new lease was negotiated with the land owners.

When work was carried out on re - surfacing the station yard in 1996 the original wheelwright's round was left *in situ* and covered over with tarmac in such a way that it could be reinstated at a later date if required.

Picturesque Turners Hill fire station is a converted blacksmith's forge.   *Author*

Worthing

We first hear of a Fire Brigade in Worthing in 1830 when the local council mentions Mr Samuel Toller as being in charge of a manual fire engine. By the mid-1800s the town was able to boast of having three Fire Brigades, one each in East, Central and West Worthing. These three Brigades joined together in 1869 to become the Worthing Volunteer Fire Brigade, but each retained its own identity and command.

In 1892 the Brigade was renamed the Worthing Borough Fire Brigade under the control of the Town Council, there being three watches with a total establishment of 46 men and one Captain. Soon afterwards this establishment was reduced to 26 men and one Captain, all based at the main fire station in the old Town Hall, the other two stations being retained as storage points for ladders and hose.

The year 1903 saw the building of a new fire station in the High Street, which had accommodation for the Captain and three cottages next door for married Firemen. The Worthing Brigade became mechanised in 1910 with the purchase of a Dennis appliance, the penny-pinching council decided to save £15 by not having brakes fitted to the front wheels. By the late 1930s things were on the up and Worthing had one of the best equipped local Fire Brigade's in the area having two pump escapes, a foam tender with a trailer pump, an inspection car and an emergency tender which carried BA, cutting gear and first aid equipment. The nominal roll shows seven full time and 21 Retained Firemen on call.

The accommodation at the High Street site proved to be very cramped, and later on larger fire appliances had difficulty getting out on to the road. As part of a major fire station rebuilding programme the WSFB had a new fire station erected on land off Ardsheal Road, this was opened officially on 22nd September, 1962. The ground floor of the station houses the fire appliances, station offices, lecture rooms and dormitories whilst the first floor is mainly given over to the 'A' Division Headquarters staff, kitchen and rest room.

Worthing's central fire station; opened in 1903 it was not replaced until the new station and Divisional Headquarters were declared operational in 1962. *Author's Collection*

An unfortunate incident happened on 4th October, 1964 when the driver of an appliance responding to an emergency call lost control and crashed on Chapel Street. The appliance skidded on its side for about 100 feet leaving a trail of damage behind it. The five crew were surprisingly uninjured having only minor cuts and bruising, and were quickly able to scramble out of the wreckage. This was fortunate as spilled petrol quickly ignited and the engine was soon burning fiercely, the second engine responding to the 999 call had to stop and put out the burning fire appliance. The emergency call proved to be a hoax.

One call which was not a hoax was received on 28th October, 1987. The Warnes Hotel, an historic building on the town's sea front and dating back to the 1820s, had caught fire whilst standing empty. The sound of fireworks was heard just before the flames were first noticed. Worthing Firefighters fought hard to save the building, and with assistance from all over the county both wings were saved, but unfortunately the central section was gutted.

Worthing is currently home for two Dennis F88 Rapier WrLs, a Dennis SS WrL, a Mercedes Heavy Rescue Tender and a Bronto Skylift Aerial Ladder Platform.

The new Station 01, Worthing, and Divisional Headquarters opened in 1962.

Author's Collection

Diary of the Last Fifty Years

Mr A.J. Bridle, the first county fire officer, presents a long service medal to sub-officer Wilson.   *E.W. Wilson*

1948

APR 1st At 00.01 hrs West Sussex Fire Brigade was born, only seven hours and fourteen minutes later it answered its first emergency call - to a chimney fire at Horsham. The first County Fire Officer was Mr A.J. Bridle, whose brigade consisted of 100 full-time and 400 Retained Firefighters housed in 23 fire stations. For administrative purposes the Brigade was split into two divisions, A Division based at Worthing and B Division at Bognor Regis. The Brigade Headquarters was in County Hall in Chichester and Fire Control in Worthing.

APR 16th The Brigade's first major fire was called at the Keynor Packing sheds, Siddlesham. A large range of wooden, thatched farm buildings caught fire when a tractor was being refuelled. Five pumps using eight jets were required to bring the blaze under control.

JUL 12th The Pavilion, Bognor Regis caught fire when a builder left a blow torch unattended, six pumps and a turntable ladder were used to save the building. Damage was confined to one tower and part of the roof.

1949

JAN 1st At 18.34 hrs the Brigade received a call to Shoreham Toll Bridge, on arrival they found that a double-decker bus had left the road and had crashed into the River Arun. Using ropes, ladders and stretchers 11 people were rescued from the overturned bus.

MAR 20th Fire was discovered at 01.15 hrs in the White Horse Hotel, Steyning. Residents and staff all escaped but the building was badly damaged, five pumps, a turntable ladder and two salvage tenders attended the call.

APR 9th Scadgells Depository, Worthing. This large furniture depository was well alight when the brigade was called at 16.17 hrs. At first a pump, a turntable pump and a pump escape were sent , but this was soon raised to five pumps. Three salvage tenders were also called out. Smoke was so dense that firefighters had to use Breathing Apparatus (BA). The fire was finally extinguished the following morning. Damage was confined to the top floor and roof, the salvage operations carried out minimised the damage to the contents of the lower floors.

The Brigade Workshops were moved from a small bay at East Preston fire station to larger, but still not perfect, premises at the rear of Chichester fire station.

1950

JUN 1st Fire at 'Holmbush', a children's home at Faygate, started in an outbuilding used as accommodation. Five jets were required to quench the fire.

JUN 27th Camelsdale were called out to a dog fallen down a deep well. Station Officer Green was lowered down the well and managed to extricate the dog. Unfortunately the dog was found to be dead , the RSPCA, however presented Stn O. Green with its Bronze Medal for the attempted rescue.

Firemen attend the scene of the Pavilion fire, Bognor Regis, 12th July, 1949.

Author's Collection

Brigade and naval personnel assist at the Ford rail crash on 5th August, 1951.

Author's Collection

1951

JUL The new single-bay fire station at Henfield becomes operational, replacing the old shed previously used.

AUG 5th A call was received at 12.16 hrs from Ford railway station, two trains had collided. Six pumps and crews with cutting gear were dispatched. With the aid of Police and RNAS personnel from Ford Aerodrome all trapped passengers were quickly extricated. The final casualty roll was nine dead and 46 injured.

1952

MAY 16th Flynns Dye Works, Southwick. Excessive heat in an unattended drying cabinet was put down as the cause of this five-pump fire, which seriously damaged a large part of the first floor of the building.

1953

MAY East Wittering's new fire station became operational, this building is a conversion from an older Electricity Board premises.

JUL 25th A call was received at 22.17 hrs to the premises of J. Evershed & Sons, Grocers, Provision Merchants and Soap Fat and Bleaching Products Manufacturers. On arrival the crew of the first pump found a stack of 50,000 pallets on fire, and the paint on a tank containing 3,000 gallons of White Spirit was blistering. A further seven appliances were sent before the fire was extinguished.

JUL The new fire station at Billingshurst became operational.

NOV The new fire station at Bosham became operational.

1954

A call was received to a flat in Stoke Abbot Road, Worthing. Three appliances were sent from Worthing and a further pump from Lancing was called out. The fire, caused by an overturned oil heater, was quickly put out by means of three hose reel jets and one from a hydrant.

DEC The new fire station at Shoreham-

by-Sea became operational. This station replaced a row of sheds first occupied as a temporary measure during the war.

Firemen attack a major fire at the premises of the Norfolk Laundry, Littlehampton. *McMullen*

1955

Midhurst fire station is moved out of the old town goal site, to a new location at the Wharf, Midhurst.

SEP 6th Hampshire Fire Brigade received a call from a large private house in Lumley, on the Sussex/Hampshire border. They dispatched one pump under the Mutual Assistance Scheme and passed the call on to Chichester who completed the first attendance with the dispatch of a further pump.

1956

MAR 20th Following an explosion in a Calor Gas cylinder, fire severely affected a large timber shed belonging to the Austin Poultry Farm, Fernhurst. 3,000 chicks died in the fire which was put out by crews from Camelsdale.

A wheeled escape ladder in use at an East Street, Chichester, fire in January 1953.

E.W. Wilson

Shoreham fire station, Butts Road. This fire station was closed in December 1953.
Author's Collection

Salt Hill House, a large country mansion, was badly damaged by fire in February 1955.
Author's Collection

Fireman Wilson rushes to extinguish a stubble fire at Madam Green Farm, Oving, in September 1962. *J. New*

Station 17, Chichester, and the Fire Brigade headquarters on opening day, 4th November 1965. The appliances move in convoy from the old cattle market fire station. *J.W. Percy*

MAY 11th An RAF Valiant bomber crashed onto the railway line near to Southwick Halt. Small fires in 15 properties were dealt with by two pumps from Shoreham fire station with assistance from East Sussex and Brighton Fire Brigades.

JUN Crawley`s new fire station becomes operational and the manning is changed from Day to 24 hours.

1957

The Brigade Workshops move from the rear of Station 17, Chichester, to a new garage site on St Pancras.

1958

MAY The new fire station at Storrington becomes operational.

OCT 14th Fire in the premises of Jordan & Cook, bedding manufacturers is dealt with by two pumps from Worthing with the assistance of three further pumps supplied by Lancing and Findon.

1959

SEP 18th Warnham Brick Works, careless use of an oxyacetylene cutter caused a timber building at these premises to ignite. Appliances from Horsham, Billingshurst, Crawley and Henfield attended along with one pump from the Surrey Fire Brigade. Five jets were used to extinguish the fire, but the building was severely damaged.

1960

MAR 23rd 06.23 hrs, a call is received to the Rivoli Cinema, Chapel Street Worthing. The first attendance pump from Worthing quickly called for assistance as the auditorium was well alight. Pumps are sent from East Preston, Findon, Storrington, Horsham, Shoreham, Lancing and Bognor Regis. The roof of the building had collapsed before the Firefighters, wearing 12 sets of BA and using 11 hose reel jets, had extinguished the flames.

1961

FEB 9th Silver Queen Garage, Worthing. On arrival the crew from Worthing found this bus depot to be well alight and quickly made pumps six. Two appliances each were sent from Worthing and Lancing and one from East Preston. The building, containing 10 coaches and 10 private cars, was quickly extinguished and damage was restricted to only a part of the roof and a small number of vehicles.

MAR New fire stations at Steyning and Petworth become operational.

AUG The new fire station at East Preston becomes operational. Originally a barn, it was successfully converted to a fire station without damaging the effect of the building.

NOV 29th Marine Hotel, Selsey. The Officer in Charge of the first appliance found the ground and first floors well alight and immediately called for more assistance. Two appliances were sent from Bognor Regis, three - including the turntable ladder - came from Chichester and one each from Selsey and East Wittering. After one hour Firefighters were withdrawn from inside the building as its condition was becoming dangerous. Eight jets were in use subduing the flames, and because of the strong wind a Land Rover patrolled the area dealing with flying embers. The last crew left the scene late in the evening of the following day, nearly 20 hours after the first attendance.

1962

SEP The new fire station at Partridge Green becomes operational, as does the new Divisional Headquarters and fire station at Worthing.

DEC 31st Pythingdean Farm, fire in a single-storey farm building containing seven calves and 45 tons of straw was extinguished by one jet and five hose reel jets by crews from Billingshurst, Storrington and Horsham.

1963

JAN 4th Two Firemen with firefighting equipment were conveyed by RNLI lifeboat to the *Don Bosco* fishing trawler one mile west of the Owers Lightship in the English Channel. Fire was quickly spreading from the engine room to the timber decking and hull. A further three Firemen with BA were winched onto the deck by RAF helicopter. The Naval vessel *Confience* arrived later on the scene and her crew took over the fire fighting operation. HMS *Confience* later towed the MV *Don Bosco* into Southampton Docks.

Work was begun on the new Chichester fire station and Brigade Headquarters on a site at Northgate, Chichester.

1964

MAR 5th Following the collision of two freight trains at Itchingfield Junction, Christ's Hospital, Brigade personnel assisted in the rescue of the trapped drivers. Unfortunately both men were certified dead at the scene.

DEC The new fire station at Selsey becomes operational.

1965

JUN 11th The Brigade Headquarters is established in the new Northgate building.

NOV 4th 09.30 hrs Station 17, Chichester and the Fire Control become operational at Northgate.

1966

JAN The new fire station at Findon becomes operational.

Camelsdale fire station closes due to reduced calls and the close proximity of a station in Surrey. Camelsdale's ground is taken over by Midhurst and Petworth.

1967

MAR The new fire station at Arundel becomes operational.

1968

JUL The new fire station and Divisional Headquarters at Horsham becomes operational.

1969

MAR The new fire station at Lancing becomes operational.

JUL The new fire station at Littlehampton becomes operational.

1970

OCT 26th The new fire station at Midhurst becomes operational.

1971

Drill towers are erected at Lancing, Littlehampton and Petworth fire stations.

1972

MAY 31st The Brigade's first Chief Officer, Mr A.J. Bridle retires after 24 years and is replaced by Mr Stanley Crook, who is promoted from Deputy County Fire Officer.

1973

Fire at Datsuns, Lancing. The old Lancing Carriage Works, now used as the premises of Datsun UK are seriously damaged by fire. Much of the warehouse is destroyed before the fire is put out.

1974

County boundary changes bring six more fire stations under the control of the Brigade. They are retained stations at Turners Hill, Burgess Hill, Keymer and Hurstpierpoint and day manning stations at East Grinstead and Haywards Heath.

MAY 10th Beves Timber Yard, Shoreham. Fire involving a large stack of timber, a treatment shed and several tanks containing 1,500 gallons of fuel oil and 4,000 gallons of wood preservatives. The fire was extinguished by the use of ten jets, one hydraulic platform monitor and foam from three 5X foam branches. Twelve pumps, one HP, two Land Rover appliances, one foam carrier, one BA control vehicle and a control unit attended the incident.

Firefighters from all over the county were called to the Datsun warehouse fire, Lancing.
Author's Collection

1975

AUG 12th The Brigade was called to an Emergency Special Service on Shoreham beach where a 16-year-old boy was in danger of drowning whilst being trapped up to his neck in sand and shingle. He had dug a hole in the beach just below the high water mark which the incoming tide had caused to collapse around him. Efforts to release him by brigade, Police and Ambulance Service personnel by digging and pulling did not work as new shingle immediately fell back in the hole from the action of the tide. As the water level rose the boy was provided with a BA set to enable him to breath with his head under water. He was finally extricated with the aid of a mechanical digger and by firemen using a large jet to agitate the shingle and releasing the suction around the boy's body.

DEC The new fire station at Bognor Regis becomes operational. This replaced an earlier town centre station from which it was difficult to respond to calls during the heaviest part of the tourist season.

1976

JUN 15th Gatwick Airport. The brigade was called to a spillage of ammonia in the cargo hold of a Boeing 707 aircraft. Firemen wearing BA and chemical protection suits were able to access the cargo hold of the aircraft and successfully remove the spillage.

1977

OCT 27th Holmbush House, Faygate. Fire in a large unoccupied house was fought by firefighters wearing BA. Twelve appliances attended the scene and five jets were used to subdue the flames.

NOV Firefighters go on strike for better pay and conditions, Green Goddess fire engines and troops provide fire cover in West Sussex.

Woolworth's store, Bognor Regis, well alight.   *Author's Collection*

Woolworth's store, Bognor Regis, at the height of the fire. *Author's Collection*

1978

JAN The national Firemen's strike is over and the fire service returns to normal. The Brigade Workshops move from St Pancras in Chichester to a new site at Tangmere. The building is an old RAF stores on the wartime airfield.

AUG 26th At 14.03 hrs the Brigade received a call to the Bognor Regis branch of Woolworths, smoke issuing. Bognor's retained crew responded to the 'shout', it very quickly became obvious that this was a major fire and help was called for. Twice the attendance was raised, including a call for Worthing's hydraulic platform. At 14.52 hrs the call was raised to make pumps 20. At the height of the fire up to 35 appliances and over 160 Firefighters were in action. Including relief crews, 70 appliances, some supplied by Hampshire and Surrey Fire Brigades, attended the call before the stop message was sent. Eleven Firefighters were taken to hospital suffering from minor injuries or exhaustion. Damage was restricted to the Woolworth's building, but at a cost of £2 million.

Firefighters attack the fire at Woolworth's store, Bognor Regis. *Author's Collection*

The spire of Cuckfield parish church 'well alight'. *I. Henley*

1979

DEC 26th Southern Hanger, Laker Airways Gatwick Airport. Fire in this maintenance hanger was fought by crews of four appliances using six jets. Aircraft and buildings close by were kept cool using jets operating from the service roadway.

1980

MAY 1st The spire of the 15th century parish church at Cuckfield was severely damaged by fire. Firefighters from Burgess Hill, Haywards Heath and Horsham using three jets managed to prevent the fire spreading to the roof space, and the Horsham hydraulic platform attacked the spire. Due to the danger of falling embers the spire was allowed to burn down to the level of the roof before being finally extinguished.

1981

JUL 23-24-25th Frisian Star, Shoreham Harbour. On the evening of the 23rd of July the MV *Frisian Star*, loaded with highly flammable and toxic toluene, methyl ethyl ketone and Diethanolamine was allowed to enter Shoreham Harbour with a suspected chemical leak in the hold. It was quickly established that toluene was leaking out of several drums and a full scale emergency was declared. Approximately 500 members of the public were evacuated from their homes as the County Fire Officer, Mr Blackburn, took charge of the situation.. As well as the Brigade, experts from the Port Authority, Police, Ambulance Service, Chemical Industries Association, H&S Executive, County Emergency Planning Team and the District Council all took their part. The crisis was resolved when bulk nitrogen gas was pumped into the hold to displace the dangerous fumes.

The fire station at Horley was handed over to WSFB control . This station had been in West Sussex since the boundary changes in 1974, but protracted negotiations with Surrey County Council had held up the change over until now.

1982

JAN 27th A glider from the Southern Gliding Club, Parham, came to rest in an unusual position following a forced landing, balanced between a tree and a 400 volt overhead power line. Using ladders and a hydraulic platform Firefighters were able to rescue the pilot and her instructor without further injury.

Fitting out of the new Fire Control building continued throughout the year.

1983

FEB 26-27th The new Fire Control comes on line over this weekend.

SEP 22nd High Street, Crawley. This four-pump fire involved a pair of buildings, built in 1500, converted into seven commercial properties. Using eight BA sets, four jets and two hose reels the fire was brought under control in just over one and a half hours.

1984

MAR 5th Brigade personnel from Horsham and Crawley released seven cows from a slurry pit in a rescue operation lasting a little over two hours.

JUL 9th Chatsworth Hotel, Worthing. The careless disposal of smoking materials caused severe damage to a third floor room in this hotel. Firefighters from Worthing, Lancing and Shoreham using one jet, one hose reel and six BA sets brought the fire under control in under one hour. Ninety-eight residents and staff were safely evacuated.

OCT 12th Following the bomb outrage at the Grand Hotel, Brighton, West Sussex Fire Brigade assisted East Sussex with the despatch of four pumping appliances, two hydraulic platforms and a rescue tender.

1985

MAY 10th Fire in a passenger train, Clayton Priory, Burgess Hill. At 02.25 hrs Firefighters from five stations responded with six appliances and a Control Unit to a passenger train which was well alight.

Fifteen passengers and the train crew were evacuated without injury, the fire involved the first two carriages of a four-coach train. Access was difficult as the railway line was a long way from the main road down a dirt track. Initially water was ferried using water tenders, later a water relay three-quarters of a mile long was set up. The fire was subdued using three jets, two hose reels and six BA sets.

1986

FEB 7th Sussex Pharmaceuticals, East Grinstead. Fire in the warehouse of this company turned out the major part of the Brigade during the time it took to extinguish.

Firefighters from 21 stations along with crews from as far afield as Surrey, East Sussex and Kent attended at various stages of the incident. The fire was eventually controlled by the use of eight jets, four ground monitors and a monitor from a hydraulic platform.

1987

OCT 28th Warnes Hotel, Worthing. The sound of fireworks was heard shortly before fire was spotted in the Warnes Hotel on Worthing seafront. This historic hotel, opened in 1890, was being converted to luxury flats at the time. Firefighters were quickly on the scene, but the fire had already taken a good hold. For three hours 70 Firefighters battled to save the building, however, only the east and south wings escaped, the central wing being totally gutted. The fire required the attendance of 14 pumps and three hydraulic platforms. Firefighters stayed at the scene overnight to tackle any hot spots, some of which were still active two days later.

1988

SEP 18th A light aircraft crashed at Westone Hill near Horsham. Two appliances from Horsham attended the incident and used cutting gear to release the two fatally injured occupants from the wreckage.

1989

AUG 30th Uppark House, South Harting. This incident involved 27 pumping appliances and a number of special appliances, using 10 jets, an hydraulic platform monitor and 30 BA sets. Uppark House, a National Trust property, had been undergoing a major refurbishment when a builder using a blow torch set light to an area inside the roof space. Extensive salvage operations were carried out in conjunction with the firefighting activities and up to 95 per cent of the contents of the public rooms were recovered by the combined efforts of the Brigade and National Trust staff.

1990

NOV Gatwick Europa Hotel. A fire in a partly constructed three-storey extension required the attendance of 12 pumps and four special appliances. A water relay supplemented the hydrants necessary to for the six jets and two hose reel jets used at the incident.

Two Junior Officers were appointed as Schools Liaison Officers this year with the task of teaching schoolchildren the dangers of starting fires.

1991

NOV Hanger No. 4 at Gatwick Airport was completely destroyed by fire. Ten pumps, a hydraulic platform and a hose layer attended the incident.

1992

Firefighters attended with eight appliances to a thatch fire in Bosham. After two and a half hours, using four jets, four hose reel jets, six BA sets and a water relay from two nearby swimming pools the fire was extinguished. Some crews stayed at the scene for the rest of the day damping down.

Uppark House at the height of the fire which destroyed much of the interior of this historic building.
R. Crosher

1993

AUG 3rd The Family Inn, Bognor Regis. This fire was discovered at 02.06 hrs and the first crew found that the fire had trapped seven people in the first floor accommodation. All were rescued from a window by fire-fighters and the blaze was extinguished using two hose reel jets and six BA sets.

DEC 16th At 14.42 hrs the Brigade received a call from Sainsbury's superstore, Chichester. Within three minutes the first crews were in attendance, as 500 people were evacuated from the front of the premises the Firefighters were faced with thick black smoke issuing from the rear. Whilst the crews attacked the fire with jets and hose reels the officer in charge made pumps six. BA wearers were committed to attack the fire from inside the building as there was only light smoke at the time, however, only minutes later the fire broke through the roof and dense black smoke filled the premises and the BA crews were withdrawn. The rapid spread of the fire required more appliances and Firefighters to assist and the call was raised to pumps

15, this was shortly raised to pumps 25. In addition to the pumping appliances, three hydraulic platforms, two BA control vehicles, a foam tender, a control unit and a hose layer were in use along with four hydrants and a pumped water relay from Westhampnett Lake. The fire was brought under control in only three hours, but it was not until 19.40 hrs that Firefighters were able to enter the building to extinguish pockets of fire. The Brigade maintained a watch for a further two days to ensure that there was no chance of the fire re-igniting.

DEC 30-31st Heavy rain begins to fall in the south of the county and the Brigade responds to several flooding incidents.

1994

JAN 1-28th The rain continues to fall and at certain times Bognor Regis, Littlehampton and several villages are cut off. The Army are called in to place temporary bridges over the worst of the flooded roads to allow traffic free movement. On the morning of the 6th of January it was decided that to safeguard the historic city of Chichester a pipeline some three miles long would have to be laid to pump water from the north of the city to the sea to the south, to this end 10 Green Goddess fire appliances and 1,200 lengths of rigid piping were ordered from the Home Office. That afternoon the River Lavant broke its banks at the rear of Rowes Garage in Chichester. Initially 10 pumping appliances were put to work draining flooded cellars, with no appreciable effect on the water level.

Pumping continued through the night and the water level was stabilised, due to the continued bad weather and high water levels a further 10 Green Goddesses and another 1,200 lengths of rigid pipe were ordered. By the evening of the 8th the pipeline was   ready and pumping into Chichester Harbour at Fishbourne began, up to 10 million gallons of water a day were pumped from the centre of Chichester. It was not until the 28th that the pumps were finally turned off.

1995

The Environment Agency donated 48 anti-pollution kits to the Brigade, each kit contains granules and pads which can absorb up to 50 litres of pollutants. Spares for the kits are supplied as required on a free of charge basis.

JUL 26th Bognor Regis railway station was struck by lightning and the roof caught fire. A total of 10 pumps and three specials attended the fire which damaged 90 per cent of the roof and 50 per cent of the ground floor.

1996

MAY Twelve acres of woodland on Tortington Common were badly damaged by fire, six appliances attended.

1997

JUL Six fire appliances attended a fire at the McDonalds restaurant, Burgess Hill, at which 24 people were evacuated without injury. Despite two hours' hard work the roof was so badly damaged that the whole building was later demolished.

The railway station at Bognor Regis was badly damaged by fire following a lightning strike on 26th July, 1995.   *Author*

The fireboat *Pride of Bognor* and members of the local National Fire Service pose on a wharf in Littlehampton just prior to D-Day. A second fireboat, the *Windswept*, was also stationed in the harbour to protect the large number of landing craft forming up in the River Arun for the invasion of Europe. *O.J. Cole*

A line of open backed Dennis and Leyland fire appliances pump jets of water into the River Arun during an exercise in 1953. *E.W. Wilson*

Shoreham-by-Sea's Butts Road fire station in 1948. In the garages are an Austin towing vehicle (ATV) and a Leyland Braidwood style escape.   *Author's Collection*

The smart new 1954 fire station in Shoreham, with an ATV towing a Climax trailer pump and an open Leyland Escape on the forecourt.   *Author's Collection*

Chichester's Dennis F8 water tender ladder (WrL) in its original red livery. It is parked outside the Chichester fire station and Brigade Headquarters opened in 1965.

Author's Collection

A Dennis F8 converted to a foam tender and stationed at Shoreham.   *Author's Collection*

A Commer WrL at Chichester's Eastgate. It carries a 30 ft Ajax ladder and has a 400 gallon water tank powered by a Dennis number 2 pump.   *E.W. Wilson*

This Bedford TK WrL is shown in its later years, having been withdrawn from active duties it has had its Lacon ladder removed and is stationed at Worthing where it is running as a Divisional spare. *Author's Collection*

The Bedford J5, or Baby Bedford. This example was stationed at Bognor Regis, the bodywork was built by HCB of Southampton in 1958. *R. Pennington*

This Bedford S series water tender is parked on the forecourt of Worthing's central fire station, closed in 1962.   *Author's Collection*

The Worthing Bedford appliance after turning over whilst responding to a hoax call in 1964. Despite the damage and also catching fire shortly after the crash the crew fortunately received only minor injuries. *J.W. Percy*

A Bedford S series WrL escape seen on the drill yard at Bognor's Clarence Road fire station.
J. Williams

Chichester's F44 WrL stands on the drill yard in front of the practice tower, it was powered by a Rolls Royce engine developing 235 bhp.   R. Pennington

Dennis R series WrL built by Dennis of Guildford between 1976 and 1979. *Author's Collection*

Dennis D series stationed at Littlehampton, this appliance is in the Coventry yellow livery adopted in the late 1960s which lasted until 1978 when it was replaced by the more traditional red. *Author's Collection*

A 1988 Dennis SS with bodywork by Carmichael. It is stationed at Worthing.

J. Scott

Midhurst's Dennis D series, it was fitted with a 45 foot Lacon ladder and had a 4.2 litre Jaguar engine with a 5 speed gearbox.   *J.W. Percy*

Dennis DS WrL. New to the Brigade in 1986 it has a Carmichael body and is powered by a Perkins T500 diesel engine. This appliance was stationed at East Wittering. *Author's Collection*

The front line fire appliances at Crawley. They are, from left to right, a 1995 Dennis Rapier, a Mercedes 1124 Heavy Rescue Tender and a 1992 Dennis Rapier.   *Author*

This Dennis Rapier water tender ladder, based at Crawley, carries 1,800 litres of water in its main tanks. These modern fire appliances are stationed all over the county and are replacing older models at the rate of four per year.   *Author*

East Wittering's Rapier, less its Lacon ladder, is seen parked beside Chichester's drill tower.
Author's Collection

An Austin K4 fitted with a Merryweather 60 ft turntable ladder, many hundreds of these vehicles were produced during World War II.

An Austin K4 with its 60 ft turntable ladder fully extended for a recruiting display in 1952.

E.W. Wilson

Based at Worthing this ERF/Simon Snorkel SS85 is seen in the post-1978 red livery. It is powered by a Rolls Royce B81SV engine and fitted with a 5 speed gearbox. Bodywork was by J. H. Jennings.   *Author's Collection*

The hydraulically-powered boom on the Dennis Delta II has a working height of 22 metres.
Author's Collection

A Dennis Delta II hydraulic platform which was new to the Brigade in 1979.   *R. Pennington*

A Dennis 263 hydraulic platform seen outside the Brigade Workshops having undergone its
annual hydraulics inspection.   *Author's Collection*

The Dennis 263 hydraulic platform is fitted with a Simon Snorkel boom with a 22 metre reach.
                                                                           Author's Collection

A 1989 Dennis hydraulic platform with bodywork by Saxon.   *J. Scott*

The 1998 Bronto Skylift aerial ladder platform has a working height of 32 metres and is based on a Volvo chassis. This appliance is based at Horsham.   *J. Scott*

New to the Brigade in 1957 this Land Rover series IIA long wheelbase vehicle was equipped with a Hathaway 80/80 pump fed from an 80 gallon water tank. This vehicle was fitted out in the Brigade's own workshops.

Author's Collection

A Land Rover series III L4T stationed at Bognor Regis. It was used as a general purpose vehicle and for carrying animal rescue gear. *Author's Collection*

A Land Rover series III L4T, new to the Brigade in 1981 and stationed at Midhurst for fighting heath fires. *Author's Collection*

Commando rapid intervention vehicle, built on a standard Range Rover chassis with a trailing third axle added by Carmichael, first introduced in 1972.   *Author's Collection*

The same Carmichael commando six-wheel Range Rover seen at the Brigade Workshops receiving attention to its rear axle units.   *J. Scott*

An Austin van based at Chichester until shortly after World War II.   *E.W. Wilson*

A BSA motorcycle based at East Preston in 1948.   *Mr Prole*

An Austin towing vehicle with a Climax trailer pump on an Auxiliary Fire Brigade recruiting
drive.   *Author's Collection*

Stationed at Horley, this ex-Surrey Fire Brigade Thornycroft Nubian 4wd hose layer came to the
Brigade with the transfer of the station to WSFB control in 1981.   *Author's Collection*

The replacement for the Nubian in 1982 was this Bedford TM/USG 4x4 Pathfinder hose layer.
Author's Collection

In 1977 the Brigade introduced the Mercedes Benz 2524 curtainside hose laying unit at Horley. It carries 1,200 metres of 150mm layflat hose on two drums fitted with a hydraulic retrieval system; a Moffett Mounty all terrain fork lift truck is mounted on the rear of the vehicle.
J. Scott

Built by Chubb on a Reynolds Boughton Pegasus 4x4 chassis, this crash tender was stationed at Crawley for use at Gatwick Airport.   *Author's Collection*

A Mercedes Benz 1124AF rescue tender, built in 1993 it is fitted with an automatic gearbox and bodywork by John Dennis Coachworks, and is based at Chichester.   *Author's Collection*

This 4x4 Land Rover water tender was modified by Carmichael and powered by a 6-cylinder petrol engine. Built in 1971 it was stationed at Midhurst. *Author's Collection*

The same appliance, in the post-1978 red livery, with its side bins open to show the stowage. *Author's Collection*

A Fire Control Unit designed and built in the Brigade's Workshops, it is based on a Ford A series walk through van. *R. Pennington*

The new Incident Command Unit, introduced in 1996 it is based on a Dennis Dart bus chassis. It is equipped with four computer work stations, fax, field telephones, video camera and playback facilities. *J. Scott*

The breathing apparatus support unit (BASU) is fitted with an air compressor for recharging gas cylinders. Also stowed on board are gas tight suits, decontamination equipment, a thermal imaging camera as well as radiation and anti-pollution equipment. *W. Dawson*

A Bedford tanker converted at the Brigade Workshops to a water carrier, it was based at Littlehampton.   *Author's Collection*

To replace the old Bedford water tanker the Brigade purchased this 1991 Ford 1721 with a Boughton body.   *J. Scott*

The Brigade's first purpose-built Austin service van engineers' mobile workshop.   *J.W. Percy*

A Ford D series mobile service van engineers' workshop; it had a 540 Perkins diesel engine.
J. Scott

A 1990 Iveco Turbo Zeta van converted for use as a mobile service van engineers' workshop.
J. Scott

A 1991 Dennis DF fire appliance converted for use as a foam tender. It is stationed at Shoreham on standby for an emergency at the local airport.   *G.E.H. Peck*

This Dennis appliance is one of the second batch of Rapier TF202s, delivered to the Brigade in 1994. The TF202 with its square side windows can be distinguished from the newer R411 Rapier which have triangular sections added to the central pillars.   *J. Scott*

A Dennis Rapier R411, new to the Brigade in 1995. It is seen here in front of the Brigade Workshops where it has passed its inspection and has been given its distinctive West Sussex Fire Brigade livery.   *J. Scott*

The latest Breathing Apparatus Support Unit is based on a Iveco Ford super cargo 170E23 chassis with bodywork by the Leicester Carriage Company.   *J. Scott*

Based on the Dennis Dart bus chassis the Incident Command Unit is fitted with an expanding central section which when open doubles the working space. There are two ICUs curently in service with the Brigade, one based at Bognor Regis and the other at Haywards Heath. *J. Scott*

Fleet List as at December 1998

Station	Reg No.	Body Type	Chassis	Type	Function	Year
Arundel	F23 OCR	HCB Angus	Dennis	SS	WrL	1989
Billingshurst	F21 OCR	HCB Angus	Dennis	DS	WrL	1989
Bognor Regis	E614JBP	Carmichael	Dennis	SS	WrL	1988
	L83 PTR	John Dennis	Dennis	F88	Rapier TF202 WrL	1994
	N143DPX	Leics Carriage Builders	DSV	Dart	Incident command unit	1996
	P825JPO	John Dennis	Mercedes	2524	Operation Support Unit	1997
	TCR357T		Land Rover LWB	L4T		1979
Bosham	S269UOW	John Dennis	Dennis	F88	Rapier R411 WrL	1998
Burgess Hill	S271UOW	John Dennis	Dennis	F88	Rapier R411 WrL	1998
	J75 GRV	John Dennis	Dennis	F88	Rapier TF202 WrL	1992
	186 ELM	Safari	Land Rover LWB	L4T	Search and Rescue	1963
Chichester	H879BOT	Reynolds Boughton	Dennis	SS	WrL	1991
	P821JPO	John Dennis	Dennis	F88	Rapier TF202 WrL	1996
	K658MBP	John Dennis	Mercedes	1124	Heavy Rescue Tender	1993
	M478XCR	Leics Carriage Builders	Ford	1700	BA Support Unit	1995
Crawley	J73 GRV	John Dennis	Dennis	F88	Rapier TF202 WrL	1992
	N139DPX	John Dennis	Dennis	F88	Rapier R411 WrL	1995
	C351XRV	Carmichael	Dennis	DS	WrL	1986
	D556DOR	Carmichael	Dennis	DS	WrL	1987
	P829JPO	John Dennis	Mercedes	1124	Rescue Tender	1996
	TCR358T		Land Rover LWB	L4T		1979
East Grinstead	G262VBP	Reynolds Boughton	Dennis	SS	WrL	1990
	N140DPX	John Dennis	Dennis	F88	Rapier R411 WrL	1995
	TCR356T		Land Rover LWB	L4T		1979
East Preston	H878BOT	Reynolds Boughton	Dennis	SS	WrL	1991
	R336SPO	John Dennis	Dennis	F88	Rapier R411 WrL	1997
East Wittering	S270UOW	John Dennis	Dennis	F88	Rapier R411 WrL	1998
	F326PPG		Land Rover 110	L4T		1989
Findon	L85 PTR	John Dennis	Dennis	F88	Rapier TF202 WrL	1994
Haywards Heath	G264VBP	Reynolds Boughton	Dennis	SS	WrL	1990
	N138DPX	John Dennis	Dennis	F88	Rapier WrL	1995
	P831JPO	Leics Carriage Builders	Dennis	Dart	Incident Command Unit	1997
	XOT147V		Land Rover LWB	L4T		1980

117

Dennis Rapier R411, built by John Dennis of Guildford in 1995, it is stationed at East Grinstead.   W. Dawson

Station	Reg No.	Body Type	Chassis	Type	Function	Year
Henfield	D557DOR	Carmichael	Dennis	DS	WrL	1987
Horley	E612JBP	Carmichael	Dennis	SS˙	WrL	1988
	L84 PTR	John Dennis	Dennis	F88	Rapier TF202 WrL	1994
	R337SPO	Curtain Side	Mercedes	2524	Hose Laying Unit	1997
Horsham	G265VBP	Mountain Range	Mercedes	917	Crash Tender	1990
	H881BOT	Reynolds Boughton	Dennis	SS	WrL	1991
	P822JPO	John Dennis	Dennis	F88	Rapier R411 WrL	1996
	R331SPO	Bronto	Volvo	FL10	Bronto Skylift ALP	1998
	M477XCR	Leics Carriage Builders	Ford	1700	BA Support Unit	1995
	TCR355T		Land Rover LWB	L4T		1979
Hurstpierpoint	F220 CR	HCB Angus	Dennis	DS	WrL	1989
Keymer	J76 GRV	John Dennis	Dennis	F88	Rapier TF202 WrL	1992
Lancing	P824JPO	John Dennis	Dennis	F88	Rapier R411 WrL	1996
	G261VBP	Reynolds Boughton	Dennis	SS	WrL	1990
Littlehampton	H880BOT	Reynolds Boughton	Dennis	SS	WrL	1991
	P823JPO	John Dennis	Dennis	F88	Rapier R411 WrL	1996
	H197GKM		Ford	1721	Water Tanker	1991

Station	Reg No.	Body Type	Chassis	Type	Function	Year
Midhurst	F240 CR	HCB Angus	Dennis	DS	WrL	1989
	M472XCR	John Dennis	Dennis	F88	Rapier TF202 WrL	1994
	XOT146V		Land Rover LWB	L4T	1980	
Partridge Green	R334SPO	John Dennis	Dennis	F88	Rapier R411 WrL	1997
Petworth	M469XCR	John Dennis	Dennis	F88	Rapier TF202 WrL	1994
	D554DOR	Carmichael	Dennis	DS	WrL	1987
	XOT142V		Land Rover LWB	L4T		1980
Selsey	R335SPO	John Dennis	Dennis	F88	Rapier R411 WrL	1997
	XOT144V		Land Rover LWB	L4T		1980
Shoreham	G263VBP	Reynolds Boughton	Dennis	SS	WrL	1990
	M471XCR	John Dennis	Dennis	F88	Rapier TF202 WrL	1994
	FPO24 X		Dennis	DF	Foam Tender	1981
	N142DPX	Leics Carriage Builders	Ford	1700	BA Support Unit	1995
	XOT145V		Land Rover LWB	L4T		1980
Steyning	D555DOR	Carmichael	Dennis	DS	WrL	1987
Storrington	E611JBP	Carmichael	Dennis	SS	WrL	1988
	M470XCR	John Dennis	Dennis	F88	Rapier TF202 WrL	1994
Turners Hill Worthing	L86 PTR	John Dennis	Dennis	F88	Rapier TF202 WrL	1994
	E613JBP	Carmichael	Dennis	SS	WrL	1988
	J74 GRV	John Dennis	Dennis	F88	Rapier TF202 WrL	1992
	N141DPX	John Dennis	Dennis	F88	Rapier R411 WrL	1995
	K659MBP	John Dennis	Mercedes	1124	Rescue Tender	1993
	R332SPO	Bronto	Volvo	fl10	Bronto Skylift ALP	1998
Driving School	C352XRV	Carmichael	Dennis	DS	WrL	1986
	C353XRV	Carmichael	Dennis	DS	WrL	1986
	C354XRV	Carmichael	Dennis	DS	WrL	1986
Bde Trg Centre	B419UBP	John Dennis	Dennis	RS	WrL	1984
Spares	KCR586Y		Dennis	RS	WrL	1983
	KCR587Y		Dennis	RS	WrL	1983
	B417UBP		Dennis	RS	WrL	1984
	KCR588Y		Dennis	RS	WrL	1983
	B418UBP		Dennis	RS	WrL	1984
	FPO22 X		Land Rover LWB	L4T		1981
	ALN240B		Land Rover LWB		Search and Rescue	1964

Glossary

AFS	Auxiliary Fire Service	NAAFI	Navy, Army and Air Force Institute
ATV	Austin Towing Vehicle	NFS	National Fire Service
BA	Breathing Apparatus	RNAS	Royal Naval Air Service
BTC	Brigade Training Centre	RTA	Road Traffic Accident
ESFB	East Sussex Fire Brigade	SVE	Service Van Engineer
GPO	General Post Office	UDC	Urban District Council
HP	Hydraulic Platform	WrL	Water Tender Ladder
L4T	Land Rover 4x4 Tender	WSFB	West Sussex Fire Brigade
LPG	Liquid Petroleum Gas		

References

Newspapers
Adur Herald
Bognor Regis Observer
Bognor Regis Post
Chichester Observer
Chichester Promoter
Crawley Advertiser
Crawley Observer
Daily Mail
Daily Mirror
East Grinstead Courier
East Grinstead Observer
Evening Argus
Mid Sussex Times
Shoreham Herald
The News, Portsmouth
West Sussex County Times
West Sussex Gazette
Worthing Gazette
Worthing Herald

Periodicals
Fire Brigade Handbook
Fire Cover Informative
In Attendance
On the Bell
Turnout

Official Reports
West Sussex County Council Press Releases
West Sussex Fire Brigade Annual Reports
West Sussex Fire Brigade Monthly Bulletin